"Life moves pretty fast. If you don't stop to look around once in a while, you could miss it."

– Ferris Bueller

Dedication

This book is dedicated to my best friend, Dex, who passed in 2008 and had the greatest smile the world has ever known; John Hughes, who shaped and formed my teenage years and is the reason I will always wax nostalgic for the 80s; Ferris Bueller for always reminding me to embrace every day; those 80s boardwalk arcades that took all of my quarters during my summer quest to solve *Dragons Lair* but taught me to never give up; my amazing family and incredible friends for their unwavering support; and to everyone out there who dreams big. Dream bigger. And then make it your reality.

Table of Contents

Preface

"Dear Mr. Vernon: We accept the fact that we had to sacrifice a whole Saturday in detention for whatever it is we did wrong. But we think you're crazy for making us write an essay telling you who we think we are. You see us as you want to see us: in the simplest terms, in the most convenient definitions. But what we found out is that each one of us is a brain, and an athlete, a basket case, a princess, and a criminal. Does that answer your question? Sincerely yours, The Breakfast Club."

Chapter 1

Ferris Bueller

"Life moves pretty fast. If you don't stop to look around once in a while you could miss it."

- Ferris Bueller, *Ferris Bueller's Day Off*

It was June of 1986 and Mr. Mister, Journey, George Michael and Billy Ocean were dominating the Top 40 music charts. *Top Gun* and *The Karate Kid Part 2* with Ralph Macchio (Let's *not* discuss the 2010 reboot—80s movie reboots are for another book entirely that I just may write sometime soon) were at the top of the movie box office. And believe it or not, *The New York Times* bestseller list harkened the arrival of a novel that would come to spawn a mega multi-media franchise—*The Bourne Supremacy*.

But the real impact of 80s pop culture would be felt on June 11th, 1986, when *Ferris Bueller's Day Off* debuted in theaters. It was classic John Hughes—both the writer and the director—who had a knack for nailing the complexities of high school and what it took to navigate the hallways of our youth. The premise was pretty simple: The class clown is determined to take the day off from school with his girlfriend and best friend, and in the process, he teaches his ultra-nervous and anxious friend, Cameron, how to live in the moment. As Ferris puts it, "If anybody needs a day off, it's Cameron. He's got a lotta things to sort out before he graduates. He can't be wound up this tight and go to college. His roommate will kill him."

Ferris, played brilliantly by Matthew Broderick, begins his day by convincing his parents that he is too sick to go to school. "They bought it. Incredible! One of the worst performances of my career, and they never doubted it for a second", he says gleefully. As he looks out of his window at the perfectly blue sky, Ferris continues, "How could I possibly be expected to handle school on a day like this?"

Sound familiar? You know you did it as well. The difference is that Ferris got away with it—nine times, in fact. Of course, while Principal Rooney is pulling up Ferris' attendance records, the teen hacks in and changes his total absences from nine to two, prompting him to then say, "I asked for a car, I got a computer. How's that for being born under a bad sign?"

After both of his parents and the school are informed of his "illness," Ferris provides us with some details of his pre-planned day off via a monologue. It is at this point that he gives a pearl of wisdom that is the basis for this chapter:

"Life moves pretty fast. If you don't stop to look around once in a while you could miss it".

I always felt like that was my mantra and I thought that I embraced it as my philosophy for life. The problem was, I didn't actually embrace it at all. The day I realized it, the truth hit me hard, and has stuck with me ever since. It was 1999, and I was working at an interactive ad agency (yes, *interactive* advertising did actually exist back then). I hadn't seen my mom in quite a while, which was entirely my fault (that pesky work-life balance thing). She had flown in from out of state to spend the weekend with me. She was arriving on Friday, so we planned to meet for dinner at 7 p.m. that evening. Unfortunately, I was so caught up in a work project that I asked my mom if we could push dinner to 7:30. This turned into 8:30 and then 9:30, and I was still in my office. Meanwhile, my mom continued to wait patiently at the restaurant. Ultimately, we ended up eating dinner via room service at her hotel at around 10 p.m.—three whole hours after our reservation. Three. Hours. I missed dinner with my mom and left her waiting. And for what exactly?! Work on a website project for a company that no longer existed merely two years later. And it wasn't an emergency deadline either. The website wasn't scheduled to be launched for two more weeks.

This painful episode—missing out on quality time with my mom—marks the pivotal moment when I decided to wholly embrace Ferris' philosophy. And although I haven't been perfect, those three hours are a constant and sometimes painful reminder of the importance of work–life balance.

So, what did the poet laureate, Ferris Bueller, teach us about today's workplace and work–life balance with these 19 words?

Embrace Life in the Moment

Embrace it. Take a day off work not because of a planned vacation nor because you have a life event that needs attention. Take a day off to do something you've never done before. Do something crazy. Do something fun. Do something crazy *and* fun.

Ferris managed to sing in a parade; impersonate Abe Froman, "the Sausage King of Chicago" to sneak his friends into an elite restaurant; and convince his friend Cameron to let the trio *borrow* his dad's 1961 Ferrari 250GT California as their transportation for their day off.

After Cameron says, "My father spent three years restoring this car. It is his love. It is his passion," Ferris responds glibly, "It is his fault he didn't lock the garage."

Now, I'm not suggesting nor recommending that you spend your day the way Ferris did; it is a movie, after all. But spend it in a way that you can honestly say, "I did stop to look around, and I didn't miss it." Oh, and if you have a coworker or friend like Cameron—someone who is in a rut or is having trouble with work–life balance— ask him or her to accompany you. They may try to resist at first, just like Cameron did with Ferris, but be persistent. More than likely, they need it more than you do, and when we do something to help a friend, we help ourselves in the process.

Life Moves Fast

Life does move pretty fast. It sounds cliché, but college graduation feels like yesterday to me. Well, it wasn't. In fact, my 25-year college reunion was two weekends ago. So, yeah, not yesterday. Super-duper fast.

Don't Miss What Matters

Don't miss the events that matter with the people who matter, because these are the moments that matter most. Yes, I was reading a little Dr. Seuss earlier, so forgive me for the alliteration.

During the holidays especially, we all feel as if work–life balance is just out of reach. This is understandable. The end-of-year work demands are real and are a priority for all of us. Success in business and in life requires focus, determination, and hard work. Just do yourself a favor and don't wait for your "three-hour moment" before you decide to embrace those 19 words.

And when you do decide to take that day off, remember what Ferris said when he was asked, "What are we going to do?" Ferris replied, "The question isn't 'What are we going to do?'; the question is 'What *aren't* we going to do?'"

Chapter 2

The Goonies

"Goonies Never Say Die!"

- Mikey, The Goonies

It was June of 1985 and Tears for Fears, Wham, Katrina & the Waves (you can thank me later for having "Walking on Sunshine" stuck in your head on repeat for the rest of the week), and Duran Duran were dominating the Top 40 music charts. People relaxing on the beach during their summer break were reading *The Vampire Lestat, Less Than Zero*, and all things Danielle Steel. And *Beverly Hills Cop* and *Fletch* were at the top of the movie box office, along with the latest entry from the 80s power production team of Steven Spielberg and Richard Donner—*The Goonies*.

For those who are unfamiliar with the "Truffle Shuffle," *The Goonies* is an adventure comedy of sorts that focuses on a group of kids—Brand, Mouth, Chunk, Andy, Data, Stef, and Mikey **(Fun fact: Mikey was played by Sean Astin, who was most recently Bob the Brain in *Stranger Things 2*)**—whose homes are set to be demolished by a developer. While devising a plan to save their neighborhood, they discover an old pirate map that sets them on a quest for treasure and fortune; it was supposedly left behind by the legendary pirate, One-Eyed Willy. It's classic 80s adventure and should be viewed with other greats of that genre, like *Time Bandits* and *The Explorers.*

> **"Down here, it's our time. It's our time down here."**
>
> – Mikey

Throughout the movie, the merry and awkward band of Goonies face a multitude of challenges: bullies, the destruction of their neighborhood, a family of ruthless bandits, a difficult-to-decipher treasure map, underground tunnels with skeletons, rats and traps, members separated from the group, mental and physical exhaustion, disappearing floors, and floods. And although there are moments when individual Goonies consider giving up, they ultimately stick together and lean on the unique strengths that each brings to the group to overcome the formidable set of challenges and ultimately persevere. It is their time.

So, what did our lovable group of Goonies teach us about today's workplace?

Never give up

When Mikey stood up in front of the group and said, "Goonies never say die," it was at a moment when the others felt that the quest had become too difficult and the challenges too many to overcome. They were ready to give up en masse and accept their fate as if it were predestined. At one point or another in our careers, most of us have felt overwhelmed, outmatched, or outmaneuvered. We've been on project teams whose members felt as though they have exhausted every possible avenue to success and that maybe this particular task was an exercise in futility or a bridge too far. This is also typically when the greatest of things are accomplished and breakthroughs are just within reach. It is at these moments that the "Mikey" in you needs to kick into high gear. Take out your treasure map again, lay it out in front of everyone, and look at it from a different angle. Find the path. It's there. Never give up. Never let the team give up. Never say die.

Inclusion and Empathy

As we established earlier, our group of lovable Goonies is quite the ragtag bunch. In some way, shape, or form, they are all outcasts who have spent their younger years running away from bullies or, worse yet, running away from who they really are. But at their core, they are all really good kids with big, accepting hearts and a desire to do the most good for the most people.

At one point, Chunk—of Truffle Shuffle fame—finds himself separated from the group and is caught by a family of nefarious treasure-hunting bandits and chained up in the basement of an abandoned restaurant. Noticing that someone else is also chained up in the same room, he begins making small talk and offers him a piece of his Baby Ruth candy bar. Unfortunately, he drops the candy bar just out of reach of his hulking new cellmate, which infuriates the cellmate to the point where he screams and breaks out of his chains.

It is here that we meet Sloth, the outcast brother of our family of bandits, who has spent his life unloved and locked in the basement due to his physical appearance. He has missing teeth, one eye positioned substantially lower on his face than the other, different-sized ears that wiggle on their own, a severely crooked nose, a cone-shaped head with a small tuft of hair on top, and an odor that Chunk so eloquently points out when he says, "Man, you smell like phys ed." You could say that Sloth could have a little trouble fitting in—but not with the Goonies and not with Chunk, who accepts him for who he is and looks past all the things on the outside, which so many would have used to judge Sloth. In return, he finds out that the largest thing that Sloth possesses is his heart, and his most prominent personality trait is his loyalty, which he puts on display when he ultimately puts himself in harm's way to save the lives of the entire group of Goonies.

And this is where we learn our lesson: Ultimately, our teams and our companies are stronger when we embrace everyone regardless of their cone-shaped heads, odd-looking ears that wiggle, or the fact that they may just "smell like phys ed." It is often those we take for granted, isolate for ridiculous reasons, or overlook because of our own insecurities who have the answers to the questions, the solutions to the problems, and the inner strength to see them through to the end. Cliques are for high school, not for the workplace. Embrace everyone and we all succeed.

So, if you are in a Goonies type of mood after reading this, walk into your office tomorrow and yell, "Hey, you guys!" I've done it, and it is exhilarating.

Chapter 3

Say Anything and Lloyd Dobler

"I gave her my heart and she gave me a pen."

- Lloyd Dobler, Say Anything

It was April of 1989. I was a few months away from completing my freshman year at Elon College (now University), and in typical 80s fashion, the music charts were dominated by an incredibly eclectic group of acts, including Poison, Bobby Brown, Samantha Fox, and Kenny G. Yes, the 80s really did have something for everyone. *Rainman, Twins,* and *Bill and Ted's Excellent Adventure* were cruising along at the movie box office. And having their debut season on television were *Baywatch, The Simpsons* (still going), *Seinfeld,* and *Family Matters*—shows that had just a few memorable characters. In fact, I think David Hasselhoff is still selling out arenas in Germany.

Say Anything, directed by Cameron Crowe and starring John Cusack and Ione Skye, hit theaters on April 14th, 1989. Cusack played Lloyd Dobler, a senior in high school and an aspiring kickboxer who refers to kickboxing as "the sport of the future." He crushes incredibly hard on Skye's character, Diane Court, who is the school valedictorian and is on a completely different life track from Lloyd. While he has no real plans for his future beyond "being with your daughter; I'm good at it," as he tells her dad at dinner, she is scheduled to take up a fellowship in England at the end of the summer.

So, clearly, there is absolutely no way that the two of them would ultimately end up together, right? Oh, ye of little faith in the romantic comedy genre.

> "I am looking for a dare to be great moment."
>
> – Lloyd Dobler

In one of the more iconic scenes in movie history, our awkward but endearing protagonist decides to go beyond the chocolates and flowers to win Diane's heart. He parks his sweet blue metallic Malibu down the street from her house, gets out, and proceeds to hold a large boom box—cassette player included—over his head with Peter Gabriel's "In Your Eyes" cranking through the neighborhood on full blast. If nothing else, do yourself a favor and Google "Lloyd Dobler and Peter Gabriel." It's 90 seconds of 80s genius. And it is his dare-to-be-great moment. Although it doesn't have the immediate impact he hopes for, it does make him memorable in her eyes (see what I did there?) and is the definition of creativity and ingenuity—breaking through the proverbial clutter, if you will.

So, what did our love-struck and aspiring kickboxer, Lloyd Dobler, teach us about today's workplace?

Take the Dare

For most of us, our jobs and, ultimately, our careers are very important to us. They define a portion of who we are. A portion. Not the whole. They are typically things that we are passionate about and things we care about.

They are places where we feel we fit in and where we can find the greatest success, however, you define it.

But as we continue to build our careers and our success, we can also find ourselves falling into the old adage of "that's how we've always done it." We find a system or a process, and we continue to follow it day after day and year after year. The old faithful: It delivers results, so why not? Fair point. But does it give you a chance to be memorable? Does it get people—and, better yet, your competition— talking? Does it go viral in the modern sense? Can you put your stake in the ground and say, "Our team did that"? Probably not.

As mentioned above, Lloyd didn't rely on the old faithfuls—chocolate and flowers. Nope. He took the dare and used the great Peter Gabriel, a boom box, and a slight— just slight—bit of ingenuity to create something memorable

. . . something that would most certainly have gone viral had it been done in the Internet generation rather than the rotary phone generation.

So, take the dare. Find your Peter Gabriel, use your ingenuity, and be memorable.

Giving it Your All and Getting Well Ummm . . .

When Lloyd says, "I gave her my heart, and she gave me a pen," he is with his friends and recounting his last conversation with Diane before she leaves for England. He tells her how he feels. He shows her why he is the one for her. He does everything right. He gives it his all, and she gives him a pen. "Write me," she says before opening the door and leaving his sweet metallic blue Malibu.

We've all been there at some point in our careers. You've given the job everything you can, and you've succeeded. The project you led is having a huge impact on revenue, the process you created is making the company incredibly efficient, or you've found a way to position the business for a new market that is full of opportunity. You're doing a great job, and people are noticing. This is the moment when you just know that a promotion and a raise are inevitable. But it doesn't happen. There's an email announcement to all employees highlighting your efforts and thanking you wholeheartedly. And this makes you feel good. After all, it's good to be recognized. But it is also good—and often better—to be rewarded. And so, while you gave the proverbial "heart," they gave the proverbial "pen."

So, where do you go from here? Well, ultimately, Lloyd does end up with Diane, and what he realizes is that the pen represented her heart. It was all she could give at that moment. She was leaving for England, and her father had made it clear to her that he did not want her to spend any more time with Lloyd. So, in her quest to stay in touch with him, she gave him the pen and asked him to write her. (Remember, this was before cell phones, email, and even pagers. Wow . . . pagers. They were fun.) The pen represented the best she could give at that moment to let him know that she did care. It was her "heart."

Sometimes, what we perceive to be a slight is actually the best that someone can do at that particular moment. There could be very real reasons why the company couldn't give you the raise and promotion at that time but did want you to know how much you meant to it. The best way it could do this was to communicate its appreciation to all of your peers and position you as a leader and someone whom everyone should strive to emulate.

Ultimately, you may just get that raise and promotion, but not at the same time that you give your "heart." And if the reality is that the "pen" ends up being nothing more than . . . well, a pen, it may be time to move on and find a company that embraces its inner Lloyd Dobler.

After all, you don't want your friends at the Gas-n-Sip on a Saturday night to freestyle rap about you the way that Lloyd's do when he tells them about giving his heart and getting a pen in return: "Lloyd, Lloyd, all null and void.

Got dissed in the Malibu, don't know what to do."
And for those of you who were *Entourage* fanatics, make
sure to look for a very young Jeremy Piven sitting curbside
at the Gas-n-Sip.

"Null and void"; 28 years later, and it still makes me laugh.

Chapter 4

Clark Griswold and Christmas Vacation

Clark Griswold: "It's a one-year membership to the Jelly of the Month Club."

Cousin Eddie: "Clark, that's the gift that keeps on giving the whole year."

- Christmas Vacation

It was December of 1989, and New Kids on the Block, Bobby Brown, Roxette, and Milli Vanilli ("Girl You Know It's True" . . . go ahead . . . it's OK . . . sing it out loud) topped the billboard charts. Stephen King and Tom Clancy were the authors of choice for those wanting to escape reality, and TV delivered the premiere episodes of *The Simpsons* and *America's Funniest Home Videos* while saying goodbye to *The Smurfs*.

Back to the Future 2, *The Little Mermaid*, and *Steel Magnolias* were dominating the box office. Despite all the love I have for movies, I've actually only seen one of those, and no, it wasn't Steel Magnolias. Oh, and Taylor Swift and Jordin Sparks were born. Yeah, that doesn't make me feel old—not just "normal old" but "*Lord of the Rings*, freakin' Gandalf" old . . . long white beard and all. Anyway, I digress.

But on December 1st, everything at the box office changed when *Christmas Vacation*, directed by John Hughes, hit theaters, beginning its run as one of the greatest Christmas movies of all time. It was the third in a series of *National Lampoon* movies that followed the Griswold family and its patriarch, Clark, as he bumbled his way through the delicate art of family life and raising children. Clark, played by Chevy Chase, loves Christmas as much as Ferris loves his day off, and he does everything he can to please his family above all else.

Fun fact: For those addicted to *The Big Bang Theory*, you may notice a very young Leonard Hofstadter (Johnny Galecki) playing the role of Rusty Griswold.

Right from the outset, our lovable Clark just wants his family to have the very best Christmas ever. From chopping down their own Christmas tree, to decorating his house with enough lights to attract extraterrestrial life from billions of miles away, to agreeing to host both sides of the family for the week, and, finally, to putting a down payment on a family swimming pool with his not-quite-yet-received work bonus (which will teach all of us a lesson later), Clark is determined to have the very merriest of Christmases.

But, alas, creating a very Merry Christmas for all isn't quite as easy as Clark initially thinks it will be. And if you followed the Griswold clan through *Vacation* and *European Vacation*, you know that even the most well-intentioned plans fall completely apart before ultimately coming back together in the most memorable ways.

"You surprised to see us, Clark?"

— Cousin Eddie

"Oh, Eddie, if I woke up tomorrow with my head sewn to the carpet, I wouldn't be more surprised than I am right now."

- Clark

So, what did our goofy family man, Clark Griswold, teach us about today's workplace?

Stay the Course

Before his epic holiday meltdown (which I highly recommend you source on YouTube), when his bonus isn't what he expects it to be, Clark successfully navigates an obstacle course of holiday mishaps that make the 12 labors of Hercules look benign in comparison. Here's the short of it: a Christmas tree that is just a wee bit too big for the room shatters several of the neighbors' windows; the burning down of said Christmas tree; 50,000 lights strung across the house with care over the course of an entire day that don't light up during a grand family presentation; an overcooked Turkey that crunches like peanut brittle when eaten; a dog-vs.-squirrel showdown of epic proportions that destroys several rooms in the house; finding himself locked in the attic when the family leaves for an event and then proceeding to fall through the ceiling; a live cat, wrapped up as a gift, that is not happy when it is released; an obnoxious Yuppie couple as neighbors (Elaine Benes of *Seinfeld* fame is one half of the couple); and, finally, the surprise arrival of Cousin Eddie and his family in their run-down RV complete with an overflowing sewage tank that Eddie, dressed in a ratty bathrobe, empties directly into the street in front of the Griswold house.

Yes, our good ol' Clark certainly has a time of it, and it seems as though the universe has decided that his goal of creating a very Merry Christmas for his extended family is not to be. We've all been there at our place of business. We start with a goal that, on the surface, seems pretty simple to achieve, but along the way, we experience really unusual things or surprises that keep taking us off course, creating uncertainty that then creeps into what should have been a pretty straightforward exercise. Clark has his share of surprises as well, but through it all, he stays the course and keeps his focus on his goal of creating a very Merry Christmas for his extended family. Ultimately, he succeeds. And you can too. Stay the course. Embrace the surprises along the way, and you'll get to your goal. It may just come in a slightly different package than you originally anticipated.

Know Your Audience

When Clark does have his epic meltdown after receiving the "one-year membership to the Jelly of the Month Club" as his annual work bonus, rather than the anticipated monetary bonus that he has already spent on a swimming pool for his family, he mentions that he would like a very unusual gift. In front of his entire extended family, he states;

> "If any of you are looking for last-minute gift ideas for me, I have one. I'd like Frank Shirley, my boss, right here tonight. I want him brought from his happy holiday slumber over there on Melody Lane with all of the other rich people, and I want him brought right here with a big ribbon on his head . . ."

Well, as you might suspect, Cousin Eddie takes Clark's little rant literally and proceeds to drive to Melody Lane, kidnap Mr. Shirley, and deliver him to the Griswold residence in his pajamas. Needless to say, this was not the intended consequence that Clark had in mind when he lost his ever-loving mind, but not every consequence is intended, especially when you are communicating with a diverse group of people. Eddie heard what he heard, and he acted on it. He wasn't blessed with the ability to analyze nor to think things through. He just wanted to solve Clark's problem and make him feel better. He didn't think about the fact that kidnapping was a felony and that the SWAT team would show up at the Griswolds' front door. While everyone else in the family understood that Clark's words were . . . well, just words, Eddie took them literally and acted on them. And herein lies our lesson.

As a marketer, my job involves communicating to large audiences, and although they tend to be targeted for a specific message, as individuals, they are very different. They think differently. They have different hobbies and interests. They live in different states and countries. They are unique individuals, and this is awesome. But it also means that they could potentially process words, statements, messages, and imagery differently. Whether it is the overall meaning, the time it takes to "get it," or the emotion it invokes, you have to be prepared for a variety of responses to your message: some good, some bad, some unexpected, and some . . . well, different. Be prepared, and expect the unexpected. Every message you deliver will return some surprises. Embrace them. Learn from them. And use them to make your next message even better.

It's a great big world out there with a great big group of diverse and awesome people just waiting to hear what you have to say. Tell them all about your product or service and your organization or business, and be prepared for their responses. They may surprise you, and you'll most certainly learn something in the process, but the more you know your audience, the more prepared you'll be for how they react to your message. And if you've done your due diligence, they should react exactly as you would like them to.

One more thing on Cousin Eddie: Every workplace has one (some have multiple), and even though he may make you want to pull your hair out from time to time, he probably has the biggest heart of anyone. You may not always be able to depend on him to deliver his best work on every single project, but you can bet that you can always count on his friendship and loyalty. And while a project is for the short term, loyal friends are forever.

And if you do get a "Jelly of the Month Club" membership as a gift—"It's the gift that keeps on giving all the year long," as Cousin Eddie says—just be grateful it isn't a "Fruitcake of the Month Club." That, I think we can all agree, is definitely not the gift that keeps on giving all the year long.

Finally, if you've learned nothing else, don't spend your bonus before you have it!

Chapter 5

Beverly Hills Cop and Axel Foley

"I don't know what you teach these fellows, but they're not just regular cops. They're super cops. And the only thing missing on these guys are capes."

- Axel Foley, *Beverly Hills Cop*

It was December of 1984 (obligatory George Orwell mention here), and I was in my freshman year of high school. Pretty sure I had braces and head gear Farmer Ted style. Awesome. And, once again, as the 80s were apt to do, the music charts were dominated by an outrageous but talented mix of musicians, including the mainstay duo of Hall and Oates, 50s' throwbacks The HoneyDrippers, some Irish rock band named U2, and the modern-day barbershop quartet New Edition. Go ahead. Sing it loud and proud.

I know you remember: "Cool it now, you got to cool it now . . ."

Fun fact: Three members would go on to become Bell Biv Devoe, and Bobby Brown would go on to be . . . well, Bobby Brown.

Chuck Norris was killing at the box office—literally and figuratively—with *Missing in Action*, Freddie Krueger was doing some killing of his own with *A Nightmare on Elm Street*, and Arnold Schwarzenegger was introducing the phrase "I'll be back" into the American lexicon with *The Terminator*. Television was having a modern-day renaissance, with *Cheers*, *Newhart*, *The A-Team*, and *The Cosby Show* entertaining the masses. And a show called *The Duck Factory*, which literally lasted all of three months, introduced us to the mad genius that is Jim Carrey. Yes, that Jim Carrey. It was his first leading role, and I think we can all agree that he did OK after that debut.

Beverly Hills Cop, an action comedy starring Eddie Murphy (with a little-known and very young Damon Wayans), hit theaters on December 5th, 1984 and immediately shot straight to number one. Murphy, whose comedy star was shining very brightly in the early 80s, played the street-smart and rebellious Detroit detective Axel Foley, who is searching for the killer of his best friend, who was visiting him in Detroit when he was gunned down. His search takes him to Beverly Hills under the guise of a "vacation" and against the wishes of his boss, Inspector Todd, who is brilliantly played by Gilbert R. Hill. OK, I need to digress a bit here. Please do yourself a huge favor and find Hill's scenes online. He owns each one, even those with Eddie Murphy. Seriously. He's spectacular. And he was a real-life police officer in Detroit when he was discovered. Pretty cool.

Fun fact: The guy who kills Axel's best friend is played by Johnathan Banks, whom most would recognize today as Mike Ehrmantraut from *Breaking Bad* and *Better Call Saul*.

When Axel arrives in Beverly Hills, he confronts Victor Maitland, the man whom he believes is behind the killing of his friend, and is promptly arrested for disturbing the peace and carrying a concealed weapon after being thrown through a glass window by Maitland's bodyguards. The cops who arrest him—Sergeant John Taggart (John Ashton) and Detective Billy Rosewood (Judge Reinhold)—take him to their lieutenant, who has been made aware that Axel is in town to investigate a murder against the wishes of Detroit PD and now, of course, the Beverly Hills PD. He is warned to give up his search and enjoy California as a tourist or face the consequences—arrest in Beverly Hills and the loss of his job in Detroit. And, as I am sure you have guessed, he doesn't listen. Chaos ensues, with gunfights, car chases, kidnappings, awkward arrests, multiple impersonations, Axel having his name butchered numerous times by awesome character actor Bronson Pinchot, and one perfectly ripe banana in a tailpipe complete with a Damon Wayans movie debut.

Of course, after the proverbial smoke has cleared, Axel Foley does ultimately get his man. And despite a plethora of resources, money, technology, and shiny new toys, the Beverly Hills PD is no match for the guts, instinct, intelligence, and determination of Detective Foley (lesson coming here), who, in the process of solving his friend's murder, also breaks up a massive drug and corruption ring that the Beverly Hills PD has been trying to disrupt for years.

So, what did our hard-nosed but charming detective, Axel Foley, teach us about today's workplace?

Protect Your Team (Even If You Have to Stretch the Truth a Little)

When Axel said, "I don't know what you teach these fellows, but they're not just regular cops. They're super cops. And the only thing missing on these guys are capes," it was at a time when he and his partners from the Beverly Hills PD found themselves in a little bit of a pickle. Axel had convinced his newfound team members—Detectives Taggart and Rosewood—to visit an adult establishment during work hours on a hunch that someone they were pursuing might be there. Things didn't go completely as planned, to say the least. While the trio were sitting at their table, which just happened to be directly stage front, an armed robbery was attempted. It was attempted but not committed because it was broken up by our three protagonists.

While this would normally be grounds for an award, it actually became grounds for dismissal from their jobs when they returned to the office. So, being the leader that he was, Axel spun quite a story to their lieutenant, which positioned them as heroes, and he even threw himself under the bus by claiming that they were outside the club because they were doing as they were told and tailing him to make sure he didn't continue to do police work in Beverly Hills.

He then went on to say that the only reason they came inside was because they witnessed "two suspicious-looking gentlemen with bulges in their jackets walking into the club." Even though it was actually Axel who first spotted the potential armed robbers and, ultimately, got the jump on them, he gave his team members all of the credit to protect them when they were in a very dicey situation.

Ultimately, and in the same scene, Taggart and Rosewood came clean and told the truth about what happened, prompting Axel to say (in front of their lieutenant), "The supercop story was working. It was working, and you guys just messed it up. I'm still trying to figure you guys out. Mess up a perfectly good lie . . ." Even in defeat, which was prompted by their own actions, he continued to let his team know that he would protect them in the future at any cost, including admitting to his own lie in front of their boss. And he did it with a little humor. Humor always wins the day.

Protect and defend your team at any cost, especially when all of you are in a serious line of fire. They won't forget it, and neither will you. And if you have a good boss, you might be pleasantly surprised by his or her reaction.

Your Best Resource is You

When Axel arrived in Beverly Hills, he had his gun and his badge, but both were taken away very quickly when he was arrested for disturbing the peace for being thrown through a window. To this, he replied, "Disturbing the peace? I got thrown out of a window. What's the charge for getting pushed out of a moving car, huh? Jaywalking?"

So, here is Detective Axel Foley. No gun. No badge. No tools at all. Just the clothes on his back. And here is the Beverly Hills PD with its state-of-the-art everything. Computers (rare in 1984). GPS. Technology galore. More cops than the city of Detroit had people. Enough guns and ammo for their own military. Mahogany offices. And really clean and nice police cars that were, as Axel noted, "nicer than my apartment."

What was it that Sean Connery said in *The Untouchables*? Something about "bringing a knife to a gunfight." Yeah, that was Axel. And a dull knife at that. But Axel was motivated and determined to solve his best friend's murder and, in the process, bring down a head of organized crime who was hiding in plain sight just under the nose of the very well-resourced Beverly Hills PD.

So, how would Axel, with just the proverbial shirt on

his back, find a way to outmaneuver his well-resourced competitor? He didn't use his situation as an excuse. After losing his gun and his badge, it would have been easy to give up and admit defeat. After all, the Beverly Hills PD was loaded with the finest tools and resources.

But instead of wallowing, complaining, or giving up, Axel used the best tools he had available—instinct, guts, intelligence, ingenuity, intuition, and pure grit—and it was one hell of an internal toolbox. It contained impersonations to get into places he couldn't enter on his own, charisma to charm the right people and the wrong ones, salesmanship and confidence to convince the most experienced police officers to follow his lead, and perhaps the best example of doing more with less—one perfectly selected and perfectly placed "banana in a tailpipe." He was absolutely determined to win, and he wasn't going to be intimidated by a well-connected and well-financed crime boss nor a bigger, "badder," and better-financed competitor in the Beverly Hills PD.

Sound familiar? Well, not the crime boss part (or maybe it does . . . judgment-free zone here), but the bigger, "badder," and better-financed competitor. We've all been there at some point. Maybe it was the final job interview for a position that you knew was right for you but also knew that from the beginning, you would probably be the least experienced of the final group. Maybe it was the final pitch to a game-changing prospective client, and your small start-up was one of the final three, but your two competitors were larger, more experienced, and had very impressive global client lists. Or maybe you finally decided to venture out on your own, start your own business, and set sail in your wooden rowboat as you prepare to do battle with the superyachts and destroyers.

Whatever the situation, you are ultimately your best resource. Sure, competing against someone who has unlimited resources and the very best tools at their disposal will almost certainly put that person at an advantage, but how much of one is up to you.

Remember that big, bad competitor was once just like you—outgunned and under-resourced. But they used their internal toolkit just like Axel and became the king or queen of the hill. Now, it's your turn. No excuses. Turn on your Detroit. Find your inner Axel Foley. And if you really, really need to dig deep, I've heard that a well-placed and well-timed "banana in the tailpipe" usually does the trick.

Chapter 6

Back To The Future

It was July of 1985, and I had a summer job washing dishes
to make money to buy a super-sweet, two-cassette-deck
boom box. I would be the envy of my town. Not really but,
hey, a kid can dream.

The summer box office was heating up (wow, that's bad. .
but really it was). One of the all-time great movies, The
Goonies (please don't remake it, please don't remake it), was
successfully taking kids and their parents to a make-believe
underground world, while *Cocoon* was taking parents
and . . . well, their parents on a journey to a make-believe

fountain of youth. Meanwhile, Clark Griswold was having trouble "getting left" while taking his family on their second trip in *European Vacation*, Clint Eastwood was playing a mysterious cowboy (shocking, I know) in *Pale Rider*, and the brat pack was living up to its name in *St. Elmo's Fire*.

The billboard music charts continued their love for the combination of one-hit wonders and future Rock-n-Roll Hall of Fame inductees, including Harold Faltermeyer's theme song from Beverly Hills Cop, The Fine Young Cannibals, Kool and the Gang, and Tears for Fears. And television was having a great year, with the premieres of *Growing Pains*, *Moonlighting*, *The Golden Girls*, and *227*. But perhaps the greatest achievement in television in 1985, in my humble opinion, was also in July—July 1st, to be exact—and it was the launch of *Nick at Nite*. And why was this such a great achievement? Well, now, from 11 p.m. to 1 a.m. every night, I get to watch four episodes of Friends, and well, my friends, this is wondrous and joyful. It means that Phoebe, Joey, Rachel, Ross, Monica, Chandler, and, of course, my favorite, Janice, will entertain this night owl for years to come.

Back to the Future, starring Michael J. Fox and directed by Robert Zemeckis, hit theaters on July 3rd of 1985. Oh, and there was this executive producer named Steven Spielberg, but no one really knew who he was or heard from him again. Marty McFly, played by Fox, is a 17-year-old high school student who is sent plummeting 30 years into the past via the coolest car of the 80s—the DeLorean. Well, it is a time-traveling DeLorean, thanks to a plutonium-powered invention called a flux capacitor created by our lesson leader for this article, Dr. Emmett Brown. During his time travels, Marty unwittingly gets in the way of his high school-aged parents meeting and falling in love. He realizes that the only way to fix this and make sure that he actually exists in the future is to find his friend Doc Brown in 1955, convince him he is actually from the future, get his help to bring the teenage versions of his parents back together, and ultimately send him *Back to the Future*.

Fun fact: Besides penning and performing "The Power of Love" and "Back in Time," Huey Lewis of Huey Lewis and the News played an uncredited high school band audition judge.

As you can imagine, things don't go quite as simply as expected. OK, if that sounded simple to you, I'd like to go back in time and cheat off of you in high school algebra. Seriously, when they put the numbers with the letters? $2x+y=10$? That just hurt my head writing it. But I digress.

Marty spends most of his time in 1955 with Doc Brown as they devise a plan to send him back to the future. Although, when Marty tells him that they will need 1.21 gigawatts of power and plutonium to make it happen, Doc replies with, "I'm sure that in 1985, plutonium is available in every corner drug store, but in 1955, it's a little hard to come by. Marty, I'm sorry, but I'm afraid you are stuck here."

The only source of power that can create the 1.21 gigawatts needed is lightning. Marty remembers that the clock tower was hit by lightning, and he provides Doc with the exact date and time. At this point, Doc makes it clear to Marty that he must avoid any situations that could impact the future, and he tells him that he cannot leave the residence until they find a way to send him home. Marty tells him that he has already run into his mom and dad, to which Doc Brown replies with his now-classic saying, "Great Scott!" and the race to bring Marty back to the future begins. Although Marty is our main protagonist, it is actually Doc Brown who provides us with the knowledge that we need to survive and thrive in the most impossible of situations.

So, what did our eccentric and frazzled but genius Doc Brown teach us about today's workplace?

Answer Every Challenge

When Doc Brown said, "Don't worry. As long as you hit that wire with the connecting hook at precisely 88 miles per hour, the instant the lightning strikes the tower, everything will be fine," it was an incredibly poor, albeit humorous, attempt to help Marty McFly relax, as the moment to send him back to the future was rapidly approaching. It was the moment that would either return him to his life in 1985 or completely erase his existence and leave him stuck in 1955. Sure seems simple enough. No pressure, McFly.

We've all been there. A work challenge that just seems absolutely insurmountable. Dare I say the word "impossible"? Lots of moving parts, unreasonable timing, an untested resource, and one opportunity to get it right. It is in these moments that many of us begin to feel an overwhelming sense of doom, and some of us begin to think about our exit plans. Don't go there . . . ever. Look, let me put it this way. If Patrick Dempsey can go from nerd extraordinaire in the 1987 classic romantic comedy *Can't Buy Me Love* (which you should put on your list if you haven't seen it) to the dapper and handsome "Dr. McDreamy" in the television show *Grey's Anatomy*, well, then nothing is impossible.

Answer the challenge. If you are the process type, bite off pieces of the project and take it one step at a time. Don't overwhelm yourself with everything that has to happen all at once. Take it "Step by Step," just like *NKOTB* taught you (OK, so the song was released in 1990, but the boy band was formed in the late 80s, so it still counts), and you'll time the lightning strike perfectly.

And if you are like me and prefer the "I'll figure it out along the way" approach, then embrace the chaos, hop in the DeLorean, put the pedal to the metal, and use your *Magnum P.I.* "little voice inside" to guide you. It may not always get you to exactly 88 mph, but if you stay on top of the project and make the necessary adjustments along the way, you should be able to hit somewhere between 85 and 89 mph, and it may surprise you just how good that really is. Worst-case scenario, you end up in 1983 or 1987, which isn't really that far off in the scheme of things. And besides, they were awesome years for pop culture, so there is always that.

Be A Visionary

"Roads? Where we're going, we don't need roads."

— Dr. Emmett Brown

At the end of the movie, Doc Brown; Marty; and Marty's girlfriend, Jenny, are in the DeLorean heading to the year 2015 when Marty becomes concerned about their ability to hit 88 mph and mentions that they don't have enough road. Doc Brown responds with "Roads? Where we're going, we don't need roads."

Now, Doc Brown really didn't know what 2015 looked like and didn't really have any idea whether they would actually need roads or not. But he built his newest DeLorean time machine so that it could perform without roads because he believed in the promise of the future. He believed it would be amazing, and he believed in his vision.

It's this last part that is the most important: He believed in his vision. And that's where you come in. The greatest of our inventors and visionaries believe that there is something greater out there, but they don't necessarily know where their vision is going to take them or if what they believe is possible is, well, actually possible. However, just like our eccentric genius Doc Brown, they always speak with confidence about their vision, which inspires others around them to believe as well.

Most people follow someone else's vision, and that's OK.

But how awesome would it be if that vision was yours? We all have that inside of us—the ability to see something that others don't . . . and no, not in a *Sixth Sense*-movie kind of "I see dead people" way, although that would be super cool . . . maybe . . . I mean, if they weren't scary ghosts. And when your team believes in your vision, they will follow you, even if deep down, they also know that the journey is uncertain and, ultimately, none of you are really sure if you'll actually need roads where you are going. It doesn't matter. They believe because you believe, and this makes you a visionary.

None of us can go "Back in Time" as the song suggests, but we can chart a course for our future and, hopefully, one that doesn't need a Delorean, 1.21 gigawatts of power, and a flux capacitor to get there. Although that would be pretty damn cool!

Chapter 7

E.T.

"Be Good."
- E.T.

It was June of 1982, and I had just graduated from the 6th grade. I was getting ready to go from the king of elementary school to the king of the Dorks (so eloquently stated by Farmer Ted in *Sixteen Candles*) as I entered the much larger and more intimidating halls of middle school. And like a typical 12-year-old boy, I was going through Clearasil faster than the girls in my class went through a can of non-ozone-friendly hairspray.

With the school year ending, the production companies began releasing their "can't miss" summer movies. Harrison Ford, minus the whip and hat, starred in the futuristic *Blade Runner*, while Sylvester Stallone took on my favorite of the Rocky villains—Clubber Lang, whose classic prediction for the fight was "pain"—in *Rocky 3*, and the pre-JJ Abrams *Star Trek 2: The Wrath of Khan* was entertaining audiences with a super heavy dose of overacting. And at completely opposite ends of the intellectual spectrum were the raunchy college coming-of-age comedy *Porky's* and the poignant, artistic, beautifully shot eventual Oscar winner *Chariots of Fire*.

And, once again, the billboard music charts were as mixed up as my fashion at the time, given my proclivity for parachute pants and Members Only jackets. Great new-wave bands, such as The Human League with "Don't You Want Me?" and Soft Cell with "Tainted Love," were surrounded by the likes of 80s rockers Asia; country icon Willie Nelson; one of the original female power rockers, Joan Jett; and the voice behind the *Ghostbusters* theme song, Ray Parker Jr. And let's not forget two royals in music history—Paul McCartney and Stevie Wonder—who were dominating the number-one spot with "Ebony and Ivory."

Television gave us the premieres of two classic sitcoms: Newhart and Cheers.

Fun fact: Bob Newhart guest stars on *The Big Bang Theory* as Professor Proton, who is Sheldon's childhood hero.

Fame, *Family Ties*, and the short-lived—thankfully for all of us—*Joanie Loves Chachi* premiered as well, while we said goodbye to *In Search of . . .* , hosted by Leonard Nimoy, who also, ironically enough, had a number of appearances on *The Big Bang Theory*; *WKRP in Cincinnati* (I still miss Les Nesman and Venus Flytrap); *Mork & Mindy*, with some guy named Robin Williams; and *Bosom Buddies*, with some guy named Tom Hanks.

E.T. the Extra-Terrestrial, starring Henry Thomas and Drew Barrymore and directed by Steven Spielberg, hit theaters on

June 11th of 1982. It is the story of an alien called E.T., who gets left behind on Earth when his spaceship leaves without him, stranding him billions of miles from home. Luckily for him, he is discovered by a compassionate and loyal boy named Elliott, who does everything he can to protect E.T. from numerous factions of the federal government and local law enforcement.

While E.T. tries to make sense of his new surroundings, Elliott works hard to gain his trust, as both are in a race against time to help him find his way home. Along the way, they teach each other life lessons about compassion, loyalty, patience, when to fight and when to flee, trust, and love. And, ultimately, E.T. does the opposite of Eric Clapton by actually finding his way home (audiophiles will get that one), but not before he finds himself lying on the side of a riverbed dying with all of his color gone and the red light in his heart fading. And this, my friends, is where our next fun fact can be found.

Fun fact: I cry. No . . . I bawl my eyes out . . . No, actually, I weep uncontrollably every time I see E.T. on the side of that riverbed. The next time I cried during a movie was when Wilson the volleyball floated away from Tom Hanks during a brutal storm at sea in *Castaway*, and Hanks yelled, "Wilson, I'm sorry!" Yes, I wept uncontrollably for an extra-terrestrial and a volleyball. And so did you.

So, what did our compassionate human Elliot and our gentle alien from billions of miles away, E.T., teach us about today's workplace?

Find a Cause

When E.T. said simply, "Be good," he was talking to both Elliott and his sister, Gertie (played by Drew Barrymore), at the end of the movie and before he boarded his spaceship to head home. They were the last words that we would hear E.T. speak, and they summed up his personality and presence perfectly (a little alliteration there).

One of my favorite, more subdued scenes is when E.T. noticed a pot of dead flowers in Gertie's room. He looked at them, said something, and they immediately bloomed in full. Throughout the movie, E.T. does things that encapsulate his "Be good" mantra, and he clearly has a sympathetic bond with any living being, including flowers. We can literally see his heart glowing in his chest, which I don't think was an accident that occurred while designing his anatomy.

I'm not sure any of us can glance at dead flowers and make them bloom (if you can, we are going to Vegas together), but we can have an impact on someone or something that needs it and "be good." In the last decade, businesses have embraced cause marketing and social responsibility and have given their employees the workplace flexibility to do the same, which is awesome. Whether it is giving paid time off for volunteering, providing real resources to those in need, committing a percentage of profits to a cause, or supporting charitable organizations with the products they create or services they render, many corporations are making an investment in "being good," which E.T. would be proud of.

And if you work for a company that hasn't quite found its "be good" footing, take the initiative to propose something to someone in the organization who can help you make it happen. It takes just one person to create a make-a-difference philosophy within your company culture. Be that person.

And if you are starting your own business, there are plenty of success stories out there of recently launched companies that started with an absolute mission to "be good." They didn't wait for the revenues and growth to happen first. They tied their revenues and growth to "being good" from the very first dollar earned. TOMS (one-to-one donation for every pair of shoes purchased), Warby Parker (for every pair of glasses purchased, the company donates the equivalent of a pair of glasses to nonprofits throughout the world), and Yoobi (donates the same number of school supplies purchased through the company to United States schools in need) are just a few, and there are more coming every day. It's pretty awesome.

You don't need to literally see your heart glow to know how good it feels to make a difference where one is desperately needed. Let you and your company's inner E.T. shine through. Be good.

Go Home

"E.T. phone home."

When E.T. said these three words, they immediately entered the American lexicon forever, along with the likes of Dirty Harry's "Go ahead; make my day" and Rocky's "Yo Adrian." The difference was the meaning of those three words to the overall message and theme of the movie and, of course, what we can learn from them for our businesses and our workplaces. I mean Rocky could be a cool movie to diagnose one day, but it might be a slight struggle to figure out what "Yo Adrian" could teach us about the workplace. I'll ponder that one.

Throughout the movie, E.T. had just one singular mission— to go home. Sounds pretty easy, but think about what he had to overcome to accomplish this simple mission of going home: stranded billions of miles away, government and law enforcement agencies using all of their resources to capture him, a language he didn't speak, no way to communicate with his loved ones to let them know where he was, no food or water, an unfamiliar geography, and not knowing with whom and where to place his trust. Of course, something very easy for E.T. was the decision to follow and consume a trail of Reese's Pieces left behind by Elliot to guide him into his house.

I mean, we can disagree on a lot of things, but anything that combines peanut butter and chocolate makes my heart light up just like E.T.'s. Digress with me for a moment, and let me put it this way: I look at people who don't like the combination of peanut butter and chocolate the same way I look at people who don't like dogs—slightly askew and with a furrowed brow. A little crazy? Maybe. But that is my unconditional love for all things peanut butter and chocolate.

OK, so you could say that in front of him, E.T. had a herculean effort to find his way home. The challenges were massive and intense, and there was a very real possibility that he would die trying to make it home to his loved ones. But this didn't stop him, and despite all of these obstacles, he did actually make it home.

Going home for us is much easier than it was for E.T., yet many of us consistently put our work before our loved ones. We keep promising ourselves that we will get there for the next holiday, birthday, or dinner. We keep meaning to plan that long weekend with friends and/or family back in our hometowns. And, for some, it is as simple as making it home for dinner with the family, but even this doesn't happen because "something came up at work at the last second." Some of these things absolutely need to be handled immediately, and these are the sacrifices we make for the careers or jobs that we love. It's totally understandable and admirable. But, unless you are a transplant surgeon or homicide detective, the vast majority of these "somethings" can wait. And if they can wait, then they should . . . every single time.

Unlike E.T., who had to find a way to signal his loved ones who lived billions of miles away and then hitch a ride home on a spaceship, we have a variety of ways to "go home." For those of us whose families and loved ones live in a different location, we can purchase a plane ticket, hop in a car, or take a train, bus, or even an Uber. Can't go anywhere? That's OK. You can use Skype, FaceTime, WhatsApp, or any variety of video chat software and applications. And for those who have families, partners, spouses, or dogs (yes, I know cats are family too, but I just can't) waiting for them each evening, go home. Go now. They are worth it, and so are you. There will always be more "last-second work things," but we have only so much time to create the memories that really matter. And who knows? Maybe you'll get super lucky and dessert will be Reese's Pieces. If nothing else, this will make it all worthwhile!

Chapter 8

Stand By Me

"Alright, alright. Mickey's a mouse, Donald's a duck, Pluto's a dog. What's Goofy?"

-Gordie, *Stand By Me*

It was August of 1986, and I was preparing for my junior year of high school by getting lines shaved into the hair on the side of my head and coloring them green for effect. Yeah, I did that. Mercy.

With the end of summer rapidly approaching, the box office was still awash with blockbusters. Yes, in those days of 80s yore, movies actually stayed in theaters longer than a fortnight. In fact, some continued to sell tickets for months before eventually going the way of the VHS tape and the "coming soon" board with white plastic lettering in your local video store. *The Fly*, with the gracefully aging

Jeff Goldblum; the sci-fi horror classic *Aliens*; and the wax on, wax off of *Karate Kid 2* were amassing massive sales of $3.00 movie tickets. Oh, and lest we forget, the world was being introduced to Maverick, Goose, and Iceman in the American classic *Top Gun*.

The Top 40 in music was once again proving that the 80s most certainly had something for everyone. The classic sounds of Steve Winwood reverberating through "Higher Love"; the one-hit wonder Jermaine Stewart with his super-catchy ode to morals in "We Don't Have to Take Our Clothes Off"; Peter Cetera - who was essentially the John Williams (*Star Wars* composer) of the Karate Kid trilogy - with his latest love ballad, "The Glory of Love"; and the female alt pop band Bananarama with its smash hit "Venus." Now that all of these are in your head once again, I would be remiss not to recognize the most inventive of songs in 1986 and one that launched a new sound that is often replicated but never duplicated, as someone once said. Run-DMC and Aerosmith combined their massive forces for a rap/rock remake of "Walk this Way"—mind-blowing genius for that time.

Television gave us the first attempt at a new network since 1967 with the launch of the Fox Television Network, which immediately hit it big with Al and Peggy Bundy in *Married with Children*.

Fun fact: Al Bundy, AKA Ed O'Neill, is Jay Pritchett in *Modern Family*, which will also go down as one of the greatest sitcoms of all time.

Other awesome shows that premiered around this time in 1986 were *ALF,* the lovable Alien Life Form with an attitude, who was pushing the FCC envelope; *L.A. Law,* which was drawing in huge ratings with its version of *Baywatch* in the courtroom; and one of my favorites, *Perfect Strangers* with Bronson Pinchot—highly, highly recommended for a binge-watching session. We also said goodbye to some all-time greats, with *Different Strokes* ("What'chu you talkin' 'bout, Willis?"), *The Love Boat* ("Love, exciting and new"), Benson (with the incredibly talented Robert Guillaume), and The *Fall Guy* with Lee Majors and Heather Thomas, the latter of whom spawned one of the great 80s posters. I had one. Or two.

Stand by Me, starring River Phoenix, Wil Wheaton, Jerry O'Connell, Corey Feldman, and Keifer Sutherland, and directed by Rob Reiner, hit theaters on August 8th of 1986. Originally a short story by Stephen King titled "The Body," it was included in his book *Different Seasons*, which also spawned the absolutely amazing *Shawshank Redemption*.

The coming-of-age comedy drama follows four junior high school boys— Gordie, Chris, Vern, and Teddy—who go on an adventure to find a missing neighborhood kid whose body is supposedly located somewhere near the railroad tracks. The story takes place in the fictional town of Castle Rock, Oregon over Labor Day weekend in 1959. The movie is narrated by Richard Dreyfuss, who is actually the main character Gordie decades later. He's now a published writer recounting their journey after reading that Chris, played by River Phoenix, has been stabbed to death trying to break up a fight at a fast food restaurant.

It's Rob Reiner telling a classic Stephen King story, and the result is an introspective and nostalgic look at the friendships we all had during our late-stage childhood years of wonder, adventure, and innocence. It was the time in our lives when every summer day seemed to literally last forever and each school day did last forever. Those were the friendships that taught us many of the lessons we would later use to help us succeed in the workplace. And as Gordie so eloquently states at the end of the movie, "I never had any friends like I did when I was 12. Jesus, does anyone?"

So, what can four brazen and adventurous but innocent and naïve 12-year-old boys teach us about today's workplace?

There really are no stupid questions.

During their journey, the boys are sitting around a campfire in the woods, discussing the important topics of the day, such as what food you would eat if you could eat only one for the rest of your life—which, according to Vern, is "cherry-flavored Pez . . . no question about it"—and why they never get anywhere on the show WagonTrain. They just "keep on wagontraining," Gordie says in frustration. And then the conversation turns to Goofy when Gordie asks, "Alright, alright. Mickey's a mouse, Donald's a duck, Pluto's a dog. What's Goofy?" Teddy replies that "Goofy is definitely a dog," to which Chris says, "He can't be a dog. He wears a hat and drives a car." At this point, Vern chimes in with "God. That's weird. What the hell is Goofy?"

On the surface, it would seem that Goofy is a dog, and asking what he is would be the definition of a stupid question. But this is where we get our lesson. Sometimes, the question with what appears to be the most obvious answer is actually the best one to ask. It's the one that ultimately prompts the largest discussion and can be the beginning of a robust brainstorm.

I think back to the first acronym I can recall, which was K.I.S.S. or Keep it simple, stupid. I'm not even sure that they are allowed to use that in schools anymore, but it always stuck with me. Unless we are in a room full of Neil deGrasse Tysons, when we ask complex questions during a business meeting, they often go unanswered, or worse yet, each person tries to top the other by answering with a consistent string of nonsense buzzwords that would make Lewis Carroll, the author of the *Jabberwocky* (a poem built on a foundation of nonsense words and phrases), feel a tinge of envy. You know the person who says, "Let's table that while we drill down into these bowling pins and see if we can move the needle with limited bandwidth. But, for now, let's take it offline, because I need a bio break, so make sure to put a pin in it and ping me later." Everyone nods in agreement, and you are onto the next topic without actually answering the question.

"Stupid questions" with what appear to be simple answers create an environment in which everyone feels they can contribute and perhaps provide the answer the team or the business needs to move forward. It lessens the impact of Buzzword Bob, and when everyone contributes, you may actually discover that the simple answer isn't so simple. And this may actually help you uncover the differentiator, messaging, positioning, or product that will ultimately lead to the success of your team and your business.

So . . . what the hell is Goofy, anyway?

Goals are achieved by embracing individuality over conformity

"We knew exactly who we were and exactly where we were going. It was grand."

– Gordie

When Vern said to the others, "You guys wanna go see a dead body?", he set them on a course to achieve a goal that would change their lives forever. Innocence would be lost, and the challenges of the real world would become . . . well, real. But he also created a situation in which four best friends would actually have an opportunity to really get to know each other as they faced multiple challenges throughout their quest. The challenges were vast and varied: the local criminal gang on the same mission to find the body, some very hungry leeches, a train barreling down the tracks and trapping the boys on a bridge hundreds of feet off the ground, the accidental misfiring of a gun, multiple losses of confidence, and something all of us are familiar with from being in teams at work and with our families at home—infighting.

But what they learned along the way was that overcoming these challenges and reaching their goal was ultimately due to their differences rather than their similarities. Yes, they were all 12 years old; yes, they lived in the same small town (insert classic John Cougar Mellencamp song reference here); and yes, they all had a shared sense of adventure, but it was how very different they were from each other that got them to their destination.

Gordie is quiet, smallish, and a creative storyteller. Vern is heavyset, nervous, and very much a follower. Teddy has a quick wit and a quicker tongue but has an angry darkness buried inside him. Chris is the most complex—outwardly confident with leadership qualities but inwardly insecure due to his poverty-stricken and very dysfunctional family. He is highly intelligent but doesn't realize it. Ultimately, each found something in himself that helped the team face and conquer a specific challenge, which let the members of the group see the true individuality within each other. Because they embraced this individuality over group conformity, the boys ultimately reached their goal and found success.

Healthy businesses and teams embrace the individual. When employees are allowed—better yet, encouraged—to be "exactly who they are" as Gordie stated, it creates an environment in which everyone has a chance to thrive on their own terms. And this is when really great things happen.

One of the coolest examples I've seen of achieving a goal while embracing the individual was when a space probe landed on a comet for the first time. There were cameras in the control room, and as you would expect, everyone was cheering and crying. It was an absolutely incredible moment.

But this is what made it super cool: As they panned the room, what you saw was not wonky rocket scientists with pocket protectors and thick bifocal glasses. Not even close. What you saw looked more like the crowd at an alternative rock show. Here was the incredibly diverse group of men and women— some with tattoos, others wearing hoodies and a few with visible piercings—who had just steered a hunk of super-high-tech metal through space and landed it on a comet. Yes, landed on a comet.

I'm guessing that most of us don't land things on space rocks for a living (although we might sing "Space Age Love Song" by Flock of Seagulls from time to time), but we and our teams do have goals to achieve. And if you find that your team is achieving its goals, but the results are typically of the vanilla variety, thereby not providing breakthrough solutions and leaving all of you consistently underwhelmed, try removing any conformity and embracing the individuality of each team member.

Approach the next goals or strategy session by encouraging everyone to shed their corporate skin, remove their work mask, and be exactly who they are. You might be pleasantly surprised by the outcome, and if nothing else, it will create an atmosphere of acceptance that will make everyone more comfortable with each other and themselves. And that, my friends, as Gordie would say, is "grand."

Chapter 9

Planes, Trains and Automobiles

"I didn't introduce myself. Del Griffith. American Light and Fixture, Sales Director, shower curtain ring division."

– Del Griffith, *Planes, Trains and Automobiles*

It was November of 1987, and I was embracing my final year of high school with an ill-advised fashion statement by wearing a "Who farted?" shirt that promptly got me kicked out of Spanish class. This was followed by the dual release of stink bombs in the cafeteria that smelled like 600,000 rotten eggs, and this is not an exaggeration. The best part? You stepped on them, and they disintegrated, leaving no evidence. I still want to meet the genius responsible for this invention. Yeah, it's probably a good thing I didn't have a child.

With another pre-Internet holiday season approaching, the shopping malls were thriving—true story—and the movie theaters were packed—another true story. Ushers were walking the aisles, flashlight in hand, and shushing those who chose to talk during the movie. Today, we have theaters trying anything to get butts in seats—full-service food and beverage, plush reclining love seats complete with blankets and slippers, rollercoasters, and trips to Mars. OK, those last two aren't true . . . yet. And to think all they really need to do is bring ushers back and the people will come. Bank on it. But alas, that is a business lesson for another day or another book.

The box office was full of soon-to-be both generational and cult classics. Rabbits were having a tougher holiday season than their farm friend the turkey with an unenvious but starring role in *Fatal Attraction*. Speaking of cult classics, *The Princess Bride* was 10 weeks into its theatrical run and had officially immortalized Andre the Giant into the annals of pop culture history. Steve Guttenberg of *Police Academy* fame, Ted Danson of *Cheers* fame, and the holder of everyone's favorite mustache, Tom Selleck of *Magnum P.I.* fame were in their first week of eliciting "oohs and ahhs" with the premiere of *Three Men and a Baby*. And one of the most surprising box office hits in history, as well as one of the more iconic 80s' movies saw Patrick Swayze and Jennifer Grey dirty dancing their way into movie folklore with . . . well, *Dirty Dancing*.

Not-so-fun fact: My senior prom theme song was "(I've Had) the Time of My Life," the title track from *Dirty Dancing*. Ugh. Ugh. Ugh. Now, I must confess that I'm as

big a Patrick Swayze fan as you will find—Roadhouse, Red Dawn, The Outsiders, and Point Break—but that song over and over and over again from the prom DJ? Awful . . . just really, really awful.

The Top 40 music charts were delivering their typically 80s insane mix of historical talent and, well, let's call it "talent for the moment." On the historical talent side of things, there was Sting with "We'll Be Together," R.E.M with "The One I Love," Springsteen's "Brilliant Disguise," George Michael's "Faith," and Billy Idol's "Mony Mony." And in the category of talent for the moment, we had Pretty Poison (no, not metal rockers Poison, although they were there, too) with "Catch Me, I'm Falling," Tiffany with "I Think We're Alone Now," and Debbie Gibson's "Shake Your Love." The latter two were discovered singing in a shopping mall in what was apparently the 80s' version of *American Idol*.

Television introduced us to Johnny Depp in *21 Jump Street*. As you know by now, I am not a fan of 80s reboots, but kudos to Channing Tatum and Jonah Hill for creating comedy gold with this one. *Full House* debuted with Bob Saget playing corny and cheesy perfectly, just like he did as the host of *America's Funniest Home Videos*. Watch his stand-up if you really want to see how very, very different he is from the characters he played. And Lisa Bonet began charming all of us in the premiere of *A Different World*. We said goodbye to Ricky Schroder and *Silver Spoons*, "pitied the fool" when Mr. T and his *A-Team* got the axe, and went down to *Fraggle Rock* for the last time. And for those who like gritty cop dramas, the groundbreaking *Hill Street Blues* chased down its last criminal.

Planes, Trains and Automobiles, starring Steve Martin and John Candy and directed by John Hughes, hit theaters on November 25th, 1987. If the trailer was nothing more than those three names on the screen, this would have been enough to vault it straight to number one at the box office. That is some serious comedic genius right there, my friends.

It shouldn't be a surprise that John Hughes wrote and directed an absolute masterpiece once again. It's the story of two polar opposites and complete strangers—Neal Page and Del Griffith—who are thrust together through happenstance during the rush to travel home for the Thanksgiving holiday. Neal is a buttoned-up, very square, and uptight advertising executive, while Del is a sloppy and slightly overbearing shower curtain-ring salesman with a complete lack of self-awareness. He has a big personality and a bigger heart made of absolute gold.

Their three-day journey together begins with Del unwittingly "stealing" a cab from Neal after he has negotiated with and then paid someone else who claimed it at the same time. They don't actually meet at this point but do end up sitting next to each other on the same plane to Chicago, where Del proceeds to take off his shoes and exclaim, "Whoa! My dogs are barking." Due to a blizzard in Chicago, their plane is diverted to Wichita, where they struggle to find a vacancy in a hotel, until Del uses his gift of gab with one of his shower curtain-ring customers, who gives them his last available room . . . with one bed. From there, they hitch a ride in the back of a pickup truck in the freezing cold. It is so cold that it prompts Neal to ask, "What do you think the temperature is right now?" to which Del replies, "One."

After thawing out, they hop a train that breaks down and a bus (they get tickets thanks to Del selling his shower curtain rings as "stylish" earrings to girls they encounter at the bus station) that goes only as far as St. Louis.

At this point, Neal tries to strike out on his own by renting a car; this turns into a complete debacle, which prompts him to drop more "F" bombs in one scene than Eddie Murphy did in the entire *48 Hours* movie.

Fun fact: Edie McClurg, the actress who plays the car rental desk agent on whom Neal unleashes his flurry of "F" bombs during his meltdown, also played Principal Ed Rooney's assistant, Grace ("He makes you look like an ass is what he does, Ed") in *Ferris Bueller's Day Off*.

Furious, distraught, and without a rental car, Neal tries to get a cab to Chicago but is on the losing end of a physical confrontation with the dispatcher and ends up back with Del in his rental car. Said car catches on fire due to a careless cigarette toss by Del, which also destroys all the men's money and credit cards. They ultimately reach another train station via an appliance truck and separate once again but come back together in the very best of ways. It's an incredibly heartfelt ending, and for those who haven't seen it, I will not give it away. I'm not that guy. Nope. Just go watch it tonight. You can send me an email after and thank me for the movie recommendation.

So, what did our uptight ad exec and our slightly overbearing shower curtain-ring salesman teach us about today's workplace?

Your career will be a journey. Enjoy the ride.

"As much trouble as I've had on this little journey, I'm sure one day I'll look back on it and laugh."

– Neal Page

Throughout the movie, our odd couple has a multitude of transportation challenges (as mentioned above), but it is Neal who seems to consistently get the worst of it. Some of it is due to his pessimistic nature, which, at times, makes the lyrics from the 80s alt music groups The Smiths and Joy Division sound like a choir of cheerful birdsongs happily alerting the world to a new and beautiful sunrise, while some can just be chalked up to really bad luck. In any case, the journey is very tough for Neal both physically and mentally. When he's not being punched in the face and then "picked up by his testicles," as Del so eloquently states, or turning to ice in the freezing cold while traveling in the back of pickup truck, he is thinking of his family and the fact that he's missing their Thanksgiving holiday events due to his troubled journey. It is a journey that finds him on buses, trains, planes, and automobiles—trains that break down; planes that are delayed, diverted, and canceled; and rental cars that catch on fire.

Kind of sounds like our career journey at times. Just when you think you've got it on cruise control, smooth sailing is ahead, or any number of really bad clichés that every office has on a poster on a wall somewhere, you find your career delayed, diverted, or catching on fire—and not in a good way. You've hit a rough spot. Maybe you've lost your passion. Maybe your passion has been ripped out from under you by a bad employer or manager. And in the words of the 80s pop rock band Loverboy, you find yourself "working for the weekend," which is no way to build a career or a business.

There will be times when you feel unsettled or unsure about a particular position, company, or your professional journey ahead. It is in these moments that we can make our biggest career mistakes, typically by jumping at a new opportunity too quickly or for the wrong reasons. It happens; I've done it. It's likely that you will, too. And it's OK. When it does happen and you recognize the mistake, just heed the words of Mr. Miyagi from the original *Karate Kid* circa 1984 and "Don't forget to breathe . . . very important."

Look, we aren't perfect, and someone whose career journey is exactly as they dreamed it would be is, in the words of the early 80s Madonna, a "Lucky Star." Your journey will probably look more like the chaotic but incredibly entertaining travels in *Bill and Ted's Excellent Adventure* than the substantially less bumpy traipses of *The Golden Girls*. And this is a good thing. I mean, here I am late at night and on weekends writing a book that no one may buy, except, of course, for my mom, dad, and sister, although my sister may not just so she can say, "Ha, you only sold two copies of your book!" She's the best; honestly, she really is. But you know what? It doesn't matter if my book is a success or a failure. It's the journey, which is sometimes full of "trouble" and other times full of accomplishment.

So, get ready, because diversions, delays, cancellations, uncomfortable seating arrangements, and yes, even explosions and fires are all going to be part of your professional journey. It will be tough sometimes, no doubt about it, but here's the cool thing: They will all provide you with opportunities to learn, and believe me, you will definitely "look back on it and laugh." It's true. Take it from the old guy, you absolutely will.

Every company needs a great salesman

> "I didn't introduce myself. Del Griffith. American Light and Fixture, Sales Director, shower curtain ring division."

— Del Griffith

Just thinking of John Candy's character Del Griffith brings a smile to my face. He was the definition of a great salesperson: affable, optimistic, and passionate about his product and, more importantly, his customers. And he knew how to close. Take the scene in which he sold shower curtain rings as earrings to different women to raise cash for him and Neal to secure bus tickets for their trip home. He had the women try the shower curtain rings on and then delivered classic sales lines, such as, "I've got the deal of a lifetime for you" and "These are the Diane Sawyer-autographed versions." How about "This is Czechlovikian ivory," describing the pure white ones or "They are filled with helium so they're very light" when selling the clear rings. And perhaps my favorite, "This is a Daryl

Strawberry-autographed earring."

Unfortunately, not every salesperson is born with the Del Griffith gift of gab. If that had been the case, we would all have houses full of Chia pets, Ginsu knives, and Girl Scout cookies. OK, I actually do have a house full of their S'mores cookies, so maybe they do have a little shower curtain-ring salesperson's soul inside of them.

When we think of what makes a company great, we often talk about things such as leadership, culture, vision, or brand. Of course just having a better product or service than your competitors certainly helps as well. And, yes, all of these things are very important, but ultimately, it will come down to how well you sell what you do. And for that, you will need your own Del Griffith. Maybe it's you. If you're the owner and founder of your company, then you know the hustle involved in building your business. And even if you are the very best at what you do, someone else very important—that first customer—needs to know that and believe it.

Yeah, I know. I know. But, Chris, you've been in marketing for over 20 years, and you are admitting that the key to a successful business is a great salesperson? Sales? Not marketing? Yes. Yes, I am. Now I know that the standard line is something about marketing and sales being like cats and dogs. Wait, this is a book about 80s pop culture, so a better analogy might be Tango and Cash, Riggs and Murtaugh, or more likely, the relationship between Barbara and Oliver in *War of the Roses*. The reality is that a really great salesperson can mask your company's other deficiencies while you figure out how to make the improvements and create the innovations necessary for the business to continue moving forward.

Besides the owner/founder/CEO, your salespeople are the face of the company. They are the ones with whom your customers typically interact first and most often—that is, during good times and, more importantly, during bad times, when their relationship with a customer could mean saving a crucial account. Every company needs a great salesperson—someone who is affable, optimistic, and passionate about the product/service and, more importantly, their customers.

Yes, every company needs a Del Griffith. I mean, let's be honest here: Every company most definitely has a Neal Page or two or three, and who knows, maybe your Del Griffith can make all of them optimists after all.

Chapter 10

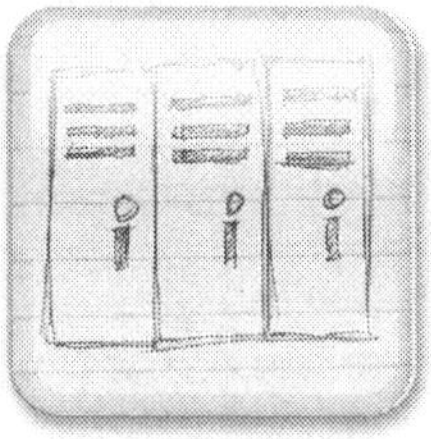

John Bender and The Breakfast Club

"Screws fall out all the time. The world is an imperfect place."

– John Bender, *The Breakfast Club*

I was a sophomore in high school when *The Breakfast Club* was released in 1985. As a typical 15-year-old, I struggled with the same adolescent issues and angst that have impacted generation after generation. I'm referring to the ones that John Hughes (taken away from us way too soon) director and writer of movies such as *Sixteen Candles*, *Pretty in Pink*, *Weird Science*, *Ferris Bueller's Day Off*, and *The Breakfast Club*—could so eloquently and precisely communicate through the teenage characters he created.

These characters and movies contained lines of dialogue that not only got us through high school but also continue to provide us with business lessons and values even today. The Breakfast Club plot is pretty simple. Five teenagers—a jock, princess, geek, basket case, and criminal—are all sentenced to detention for various reasons on a Saturday in the school library "to think about why you are here and to ponder the error of your ways" as Principal Vernon so clearly stated.

In a classic scene, John Bender, "The Criminal," played perfectly by Judd Nelson, removes the screws from the library door so that it will shut and, thus, protect the group from the prying eyes of Principal Vernon.

When the group is sternly asked by Principal Vernon about the door being closed, the Bender character says, "Screws fall out all the time. The world is an imperfect place."

So, in Bender's quest to keep his antisocial and delinquent persona front and center for the group to see, he actually teaches us two valuable business lessons:

The Business World is Imperfect

Screws do fall out all the time. The business world is an absolutely imperfect place. And while some of these screws fall out due to circumstances beyond our control, others fall out because of how we react to the one missing screw or, worse, because of direct actions we've taken to sabotage ourselves. When things aren't going as expected with a specific team member, on a project that you are leading, or just on a business day or week in general, try to remember that you do have the tools to fix the problem: patience, self-evaluation, determination, leadership, and confidence. We all have these qualities somewhere within us. It's up to us to apply them and put the proverbial "screws" back in their rightful places.

Problem Solving

Real problem solving for the long term takes initiative, creativity, and a little guts. Bender took the initiative to solve Principal Vernon's problem of prying by finding a creative way to shut the detention hall door. By removing the screws, he made the challenge of getting the door open, and keeping it open, a much bigger one than just lifting the doorstop or closing the door quietly, hoping Principal Vernon didn't hear anything that would grab his attention. And I think few would argue that it definitely took some guts, especially when you consider that it ultimately cost Bender a few more Saturdays in detention. Alas, he did keep his reputation intact, so I guess he could take some solace in that.

So, the next time that "screw falls out," just accept that the business world is an imperfect place, take a step back, and find a solution. Of course, you can always do what Bender did and deny, deny, deny, but this seems to work in politics only. Besides, who wants to spend more of their Saturdays in detention, anyway? Not me. Been there. Done that.

Epilogue

I hope you enjoyed reading these stories as much as I enjoyed writing them. Beyond the connections to the workplace today, the 80s were an amazing decade full of pop culture that will live on for generations to come, as we've recently seen in some of the most popular content today. And it wasn't just the movies. It was also the music—which was full of one-hit wonders, hall of famers, and a multitude of genres from synthpop to candy rock—and television, with the introduction of movie channels, MTV, and a still running – after over 30 years - prime-time animated series. Video gaming consoles, such as Atari, took over the world, and PCs, such as the VIC 20 and Commodore 64, had every kid connecting to modems with their home phones, hoping to find their Joshua from *WarGames*. Talking teddy bears, as well as kids from Cabbage Patches and kids from Garbage Pails, moved in on the traditional board games. Parachute pants, Members Only jackets, rat-tail haircuts, and pegged jeans were just some of the fashion faux pas to forget and remember. It was a magical time for creativity, invention, and, most importantly, the rise of the individual.

And, ultimately, we learned a very valuable lesson from The Breakfast Club when Andrew, the jock played by Emilio Estevez, said, "We're all pretty bizarre. Some of us are just better at hiding it, that's all."

Be bizarre. Normal is so . . . well, normal.

Oh, and if you really enjoyed the book and want to read more, tell your friends, leave a review online, or just email me at cclews1@gmail.com and tell me you want more rad stories about *What 80s Pop Culture Teaches Us about Today's Workplace*.

Bibliography

1. *Breakfast Club*. Dir. John Hughes. Perf. Anthony Michael Hall, Ally Sheedy, Molly Ringwald, Emilio Estevez, Judd Nelson. Universal Pictures, 1985.

2. *Ferris Bueller's Day Off*. Dir. John Hughes. Perf. Matthew Broderick, Alan Ruck, Mia Sara, Jennifer Grey, Jeffrey Jones. Paramount Pictures, 1986.

3. *The Goonies*. Dir. Richard Donner. Perf. Sean Astin, Josh Brolin, Jeff Cohen, Corey Feldman, Kerri Green, Martha Plimpton, Jonathan Ke Quan. Warner Bros., 1985.

4. *Say Anything*. Dir. Cameron Crowe. Perf. John Cusack, Ione Skye, John Mahoney. Twentieth Century Fox, 1989.

5. *National Lampoon's Christmas Vacation*. Dir. Jeremiah S. Chechik. Perf. Chevy Chase, Beverly D'Angelo, Juliette Lewis. Dist. Warner Bros., 1989.

6. *Beverly Hills Cop*. Dir. Martin Brest. Perf. Eddie Murphy, Judge Reinhold, John Ashton. Dist. Paramount Pictures, 1984.

7. *Back to the Future*. Dir. Robert Zemeckis. Perf. Michael J. Fox, Christopher Lloyd, Lea Thompson, Crispin Glover. Dist. Universal Pictures, 1985.

8. *E.T. the Extra-Terrestrial*. Dir. Steven Spielberg. Perf. Dee Wallace, Henry Thomas, Drew Barrymore, Peter Coyote. Dist. Universal Pictures, 1982.

9. *Stand by Me*. Dir. Rob Reiner. Perf. Wil Wheaton, River Phoenix, Corey Feldman, Jerry O'Connell, Keifer Sutherland. Dist. Columbia Pictures, 1986.

10. *Planes, Trains and Automobiles*. Dir. John Hughes. Perf. Steve Martin, John Candy, Laila Robins. Dist. Paramount Pictures, 1987.